Introduction

Hypnosis – what does the very mention of the word brings to our mind? If the first image you think of is that of charlatans claiming they can control your mind just by asking you to look into your eyes, I completely understand where you get the idea from. The evil mentalist who puts people in a trance and gets them to commit acts against their will has become such a cliché in pop culture and media, giving the practice a bad rep.

It is suffice to say that hypnosis is the most misunderstood of practices. Those whose only exposure to it is from stage shows and works of fiction may not have an idea of what hypnosis can do for them, when done properly by the right practitioner. I should mention here that hypnosis did after all earn recognition in the medical field, where it is widely practice. As you would soon learn in this volume, we have all been under hypnosis in one way or another. In fact, no one with a consciousness is ever free from being hypnotized. I do not say that to scare you – quite the contrary.

In the chapters that follow, I am going to take you by the hand into the world of hypnosis. You will discover what the practice is all about and what it is not. Most importantly, you will learn about how it is in fact a powerful tool that can help you in many aspects of your life, and of course, you will learn how to do it. I will break it down for you in easy to follow steps, and with practice, you will find that hypnosis is more than accessible to you. I am not going to make you the farfetched promise that you will become a master hypnotist just by reading the book. That would have to take years of practice and study to accomplish. What you will have by the end of this book is the know-how to use hypnosis to help yourself and others in an ethical way.

Hypnosis is a very powerful tool. It is not a party trick for you to impress people, but as a means to help you achieve mastery of your mind, and subsequently your life. It would not be too much of an exaggeration for me to say the hypnosis is a form of super power. What can be more powerful than having absolute mastery over your mind? You can only imagine what you can accomplish. I hope you are ready to discover and obtain that super power for yourself!

Legal & Disclaimer

TABLE OF CONTENTS

Chapter 1

The Basics of Hypnosis

You have probably encountered hypnosis somewhere in the realm of fiction. Typically, the scene will play out as such: a mentalist whispers to a trusting subject to put them in a state of trance. The hypnotized subject then willingly obeys every command from the hypnotist. If you are a hardcore movie buff, the name Svengali may come to mind. In George du Maurier's 1895 gothic horror novel, *Trillby*, the evil villain Svengali uses hypnosis to transform the titular character, young tone deaf English girl, into a singer. He keeps her in a hypnotized state, where he can continue to control and exploit her.

It may be scary to think there are people out there skilled in the art of thought control who can say a few words and make others their mind slaves, isn't it? Or perhaps you could be thinking, "Cool! How can I learn that trick?" You may also be among those who are skeptical and don't believe hypnosis is possible.

Well, the practice of hypnosis is real. In fact, it is accepted and recognized in the health care field as a valid form of medical procedure. The good news is, unlike surgery and other forms of intrusive procedures which would require that you are a trained professional to perform, practical hypnosis techniques can be practiced by anyone, and that is what you will be learning. Before I explaining the various hypnosis techniques and how you can use them to benefit yourself and others, let's begin by covering the basics and demystify the art of hypnosis.

Separating Fact from Fiction

I will say this upfront: In real life, the practice of hypnosis is nothing like the usually overdramatized depictions in the world of make belief. So, let's address some of the common misconceptions and get it out of the way. Here are all the things that hypnosis is not:

<u>MYTH:</u> Hypnosis is black magic

<u>FACT:</u> There is absolutely no hocus-pocus involved in the practice. Hypnosis has been successfully used in the medical field since the 1950s. Although trance states similar to being hypnotized has been seen and used by shamans and faith healers in rituals of many cultures around the world, there is a scientific basis to it. I will explain this in further detail in Chapter 2.

MYTH: **A skilled hypnotist can put anyone under mind control**

FACT: If you are thinking about learning hypnosis so that you can control and manipulate the minds of other, you are going to be disappointed. On the other hand, if you are wary about being hypnotized, let me assure you that you have nothing to fear. We have already established that hypnosis as depicted in fiction is inaccurate and exaggerated, but what stage hypnotists? I'm talking about the people who can pick a random member from the audience, put them under hypnosis and then make them quack and waddle like a duck for laughs. But stage hypnotists are first and foremost entertainers, like illusionists. The volunteers they call on stage are not really random strangers at all, but are either their accomplices in the act or someone who is highly hypnotizable (more on this in Chapter 5). This brings me to the most important fact about hypnosis: no one can be hypnotized against their will.

MYTH: With hypnosis, other forms of treatment and medication can be bypassed

FACT: The practice of hypnotherapy – a form of psychotherapy that uses hypnosis as part of the process – has been proven to be an effective treatment against many conditions, from chronic pain and allergy to anxiety and depression, even bad habits and low self-esteem. In certain cases, especially for emotional based conditions, it is even recommended as the first line of treatment. However, it does have its limitations and cannot entirely substitute all forms of treatment. Since hypnosis deals with the mind, it is best used for health conditions that stems from the mind, and has no physiological basis. Conditions such as anxiety disorder, depression, paranoia, chronic stress and addiction can benefit tremendously from hypnotherapy. Still, in most cases, hypnosis can be a wonderful complement to any treatment plan. You cannot hypnotize away a tumor or broken bone, but you can use hypnosis techniques to manage the pain and be mentally prepared for surgery.

<u>MYTH</u>: Hypnosis is dangerous, because it can mess with your mind

<u>FACT</u>: Precaution should be taken if you intend to use hypnosis to help with serious mental conditions. In such cases, a professional certified hypnotherapist should be consulted. For many other things, simple hypnosis is perfectly safe.

<u>MYTH</u>: Hypnosis is a form of meditative state

<u>FACT</u>: Although brainwaves measured during both meditation and hypnosis is similar, both are different activities, with different goals. The goal of meditation is to enter an altered state and focus inwards, on yourself. Meanwhile, the objective of hypnosis is to enter the same altered state and then receive suggestions, so that you can change a thought, behavior or habit.

<u>MYTH:</u> Hypnosis is akin to sleep

<u>FACT:</u> This is a misconception that had prevailed for centuries, due to the term *hypnosis* originating from the Greek word for sleep, *hypnos*. During sleep, your mind drifts off and unless stirred, have little to no awareness of your surroundings. On the outside, hypnosis can look like sleep because a person being put under may appear to be relaxed, with their eyes closed. Even so, the person is actually alert and able to register what goes on in their surroundings.

<u>MYTH:</u> Being hypnotized is just being put into a deeply relaxed state

<u>FACT:</u> While it is easier for someone to be hypnotized while in a calm and relaxed state, it is actually not necessary. As you will learn later on, hypnosis can be done under any emotional state. Still, you want to be hypnotized when you are calm for a pleasant experience.

<u>**MYTH:**</u> **You can be hypnotized without being aware of it**

<u>**FACT:**</u> Of all the many myths of hypnosis, this one does have a tiny ounce of truth. You may be surprised to find out that hypnosis is actually a more natural part of life than you think. Hold on…you may be thinking, doesn't this contradict what was said earlier about how you cannot use hypnosis to control the thoughts of others? Well, not quite, which leads me to the next point…

You are Being Hypnotized Right Now!

When I say you can be hypnotized without knowing it, I meant we have all been in some sort of situation where we are unaware of sublime messages and suggestions being inputted into our minds. These messages form a thought blue print that influences the way we think, behave, and the choices we make.

In fact, our earliest encounter with hypnosis is from our parents and guardian figures. Think about all the stuff you were repeatedly told as a child; what you should and shouldn't do, according to your parents. Now, reflect on some of the habits, beliefs, and values you have cultivated during your childhood, which mom and dad had instilled upon you and still impacts your thought process in some way. A child's impressionable mind receives verbal and visual input they are exposed to indiscriminately. Thus, the information and ideas imparted into us during our formative years became deeply ingrained into our psychology that it can be very hard to unlearn, even during adulthood. This is due to our minds' capabilities of forming mental associations.

To put it simply, when something happens to us, our mind would record it and come up with some sort of behavior as a response. Each time we encounter the similar situation, all the physical and emotional reactions we associate with the memory gets dredged up. To give you an example, I invite you to consider the first things that come to mind when I ask you to think about a rose. Think about the flower's striking color, the softness of its petals, its fragrance and its thorny stem – what sort of feelings does that imagery evoke in you? You may recall a pleasant experience, perhaps someone presented you with a bouquet of roses one Valentine's day. You may think of a person who has a preference for floral scented perfume. The scent, sight and texture of a rose may bring up a warm fuzzy feeling of being loved and adored. This means you have a positive association with the flower.

But mental associations can also be negative. Going back to the rose example, let me tell you a well-known case often cited as an example of how even physical conditions can start in the mind. There was a woman who was allergic to roses that whenever she came in contact with the flower, rashes would break out all over her skin. Naturally, doctors assumed that she was adverse to the chemical compounds of the flower. One day, as she was visiting a friend, she walked into a room where there was a bouquet of roses in vase. As expected, she got an allergic reaction…only to find out the roses were plastic. To get to the bottom of the matter, she visited a hypnotherapist who put her in a trance, and guided her to remember the events that led to her developing the allergy. It was then discovered that her rose aversion was a result of a suppressed childhood memory. It turned out that when this woman was a child, she once reached for a vase of roses she wasn't supposed to touch, causing the vase to fall off the shelf. She was severely scolded for it and the memory latched on, thus creating a negative mental association with roses. If left unchecked, the negative mental associations we develop can manifest in the formation of bad habits, addiction and even physical illnesses.

You may be thinking that if a child's mind can be easily programmed, surely an adult capable of thinking for themselves will know when their thoughts are being influenced. We would then be able to put up resistance since, as I said earlier, no one can be hypnotized against their will, right? While it is certainly true that no one can impart thoughts and suggestion to make you think and act a certain way, they can certainly influence your mind. If the influence is strong enough, then you may be compelled to act out on your own free will according to how someone else wanted. You need not look too far for an example of this form of hypnosis. They are everywhere; they show up on TV along with your favorite shows, you hear them in the radio between your favorite songs, when you are reading a news article online, they are right there on the corner and calling out to be clicked. I am talking about advertisements. Indeed, advertisers are the best hypnotists!

There is a reason why a certain brand tends pop up in your mind whenever you thought of something. Advertisers are experts in using hypnotic scripts and imagery to seep into the corner of our minds and gradually imprinting their brand name, slogan and visuals into our subconscious. While it is technically true that you can be conscious of the fact that you are being hypnotized and resist it, the truth is to always be on guard takes a substantial amount of mental energy. But as I've said earlier, no one can use hypnosis to override the free will of a person. Try think of a place to eat, a high end smartphone, an effective skincare product or a classy handbag; what brand name comes to mind immediately? Now, does that mean you would really go out to buy those stuff? Not unless you really want to, right? The point I'm trying to make here is you can be hypnotized into thinking and believing something, but ultimately, it is still up to you to act on it. Hence, you have absolutely nothing to fear about hypnosis. If you can break away from a clever sales pitch, you can break out of being hypnotized anytime.

So, What Exactly is Hypnosis?

Now that you know hypnosis is not a trick used by charlatans and there is not sorcery involved, your curiosity is probably pique and you want to know how it works, right? You may still be wondering, what exactly is hypnosis? Various researches have been conducted in an attempt to understand the neurological process that makes hypnosis possible. So far, the researchers have come up short in finding an answer. There are several theories, with some contradicting others. I am not going to bother getting into them in detail as they would only serve to confuse you further.

We've already established what hypnosis is not. So, all you need to know going forth is that hypnosis is a tool that you can utilize to help yourself and others in many ways, by tapping into the power of the mind. How effective you can utilize this tool depends on two key factors:

1) The ability of the hypnotist

2) The cooperativeness of the person being hypnotized

Why Get Hypnotized?

Now that I have (hopefully) set your mind at ease, I have one last thing to tell you and that is the reason why you should learn hypnosis. The simple answer is this powerful tool can be used to improve your life in many ways. With hypnosis, you can:

- **Enhance your overall health and well-being.** Let's not forget that hypnosis is considered a treatment option for certain health conditions, especially when it has to do with the mind. Perhaps you have a habit that is detrimental to your overall well-being that you need to kick, or maybe you just can't seem to stick to a weight loss plan long enough. Do you suffer from some form of anxiety or chronic pain? Hypnosis can help get you there.

- **Overcome barriers.** When done right, hypnosis can work wonders in helping you get over the fear of public speaking, nightmares, and any irrational fears that are holding you back from doing something you enjoy. You can also use hypnosis to prepare for distressing and fearful situations, such as surgery, child birth and even getting a tattoo!

- **Improve a skill.** Whether it is better concentration, improving your golf game or managing your time better, hypnosis allows you to maximize your mental faculties.

Chapter 2

How does it Work?

When the mind is under hypnosis, you are in a state of deep concentration. In a hypnotic state, the conscious mind that is responsible for critical thinking, judgment and analysis is turned off, allowing the subconscious to absorb information without question. Basically, the goal of being hypnotized is to bring the mind into a less resistant state, where one is open to suggestions that can change their life. It is when you are in a state of being highly suggestible that new ideas are introduces to be absorbed into your subconscious and become part of your thinking. Suggestion implanted during hypnosis can be in the form of affirmative statements or guided visualization.

With hypnosis, you can give new meaning to old ideas, beliefs and attitudes. This process is known in hypnotherapy as reframing. To help you better understand this concept, I will explain it in a metaphorical sense.

Imagine a painting in a thick antique wooden frame hanging on your wall. One day, as you go about spring cleaning and redecorating your home, you take one look at the painting and sigh. What an eye sore! You think to yourself. The picture looks dull and uninspiring against you vibrant new modern décor. Yet, because it is a family heirloom, you cannot simply throw it away. So, what can you do? You take it to get a new slick red frame that goes with your decorating theme. When you bring home the painting in its brand new frame and hang it in the same spot, it suddenly seems different, as if it belongs there as it fits in perfectly with the decor. You begin to notice the painting's brighter and more colorful spots, and thought to yourself, hey, this is actually a lovely work of art! Why didn't I notice it before? It is still the exact same painting, but you are not looking at it in a new, more favorable light, thanks to the new frame.

Technically, we can make the conscious decision and effort to reframe any experience on our own, but it if you are dealing with a deeply ingrained belief system or behavior, it would require superhuman effort to do so. That is where hypnosis comes in. You can learn to look at things from a new perspective with less resistance and strive, instead of getting frustrated with yourself for constantly slipping back into your old ways. Hypnosis can get you to believe vegetables are delicious and make you want to include more of them in your diet. You can start to think that exercise is enjoyable, tomorrow's presentation is nothing to be nervous about and being stuck in a traffic crawl is relaxing.

Of course, throughout the hypnotic experience, you are in total control of yourself. You can speak, move, and come out of the hypnosis. You cannot remain hypnotized any longer than you want to be. It is ultimately up to you to let hypnosis help you, because you are in charge of deciding what you want to reframe.

Can anyone be Hypnotized?

I hope that by now, you are intrigue and excited to begin using hypnosis to improve areas of your life, and help others along the way. We will be getting that part in the next chapter, but before that, there are two more important questions to address. If you are skeptical about hypnosis to begin with, you may be wondering whether it will actually work for you. What if you have a strong mind and are too much of a control freak to be able to set aside your critical thinking cap?

Well, remember who I told you are the best hypnotists ever? That's right! It's no exaggeration to say that none of us are ever free of being hypnotized. If you are still not convinced at this point, let me give you a few more examples. Have you ever find yourself in any of these situations?

- You became so engrossed in reading a book that you missed hearing the doorbell or phone ring.

- You are watching a TV show that imagined yourself being part of the action, until you didn't hear your name being called.

- You are so focus on a task that you forgot you put the kettle on the stove to boil water.

- After seeing an infomercial, you feel the urge to whip out your credit card and call the number.

Those are examples of being hypnotized without realizing it. I am sure you can think of a few more of your own. The bottom line is, hypnosis makes you intensely focused on one particular thing, to the exclusion of everything else. In summation, as long as you are able to achieve concentration, you are hypnotizable.

I should remind you once again that hypnosis is only possible when you are a willing participant. So, if you hear suggestions that don't sit well with your values or know it can be dangerous to follow through, you can always come out of the hypnotic state or choose to block them out from your mind. Just like you can watch a commercial over and over again, with the jingle stuck in your head, but it still can't make you buy a product you have no use for.

Can anyone Perform Hypnosis?

In theory, anyone can become a hypnotist. Being able to conduct hypnosis is a learned skill that can be honed through practice. Researchers have some differing opinions about this, although they generally agree that with practice, anyone can achieve a degree of mastery as a hypnotist. Some experts believing that certain personality traits can predict a person's inborn talent for hypnosis. I am talking about your ability to benefit from being hypnotized as well as to learn how to hypnotize, since both are related as you will learn in the next chapter, when I guide you through self-hypnosis.

You are considered to be a gifted for hypnosis if you have the following personality traits:

- You are highly empathetic as you tend to wince and "feel" pain when seeing others in pain.

- You react emotionally to daily events, even when it doesn't affect you directly and personally.

- You have excellent memory.

- You tend to trust people in positions of authority.

- You are typically nonjudgmental and not too critical.

On the other hand, you probably have a lesser talent for hypnosis if:

- You are very organized.

- You remain aware of your surroundings, even when you are concentrating on something.

- You tend to be critical of others and don't easily trust people

- You like to learn about processes to understand how things work.

- You often act more logical and analytical than emotional.

I believe that regardless of your personality type, with working knowledge and consistent practice, you can have some degree of success with hypnosis. So, worry not if you believe you fall under the lesser talented group; you just need to practice a little bit more, learn to be less resistant when you need to use hypnosis, and trust yourself. There is no better way to learn hypnosis techniques and get right into practicing them than on yourself. In the next chapter, you will learn to do just that.

Chapter 3

Let's Start with Yourself!

This is the meat and beans chapter! You are about to learn simple, yet effective and powerful hypnosis techniques and how to apply them to better your life, and to help others out. It is important that you familiarize yourself with the principles and techniques laid out here, and practice it every day by yourself. So, I encourage you to take your time and come back to this chapter as often as needed.

Let me start off by telling you a little more about self-hypnosis. Think about what it would be like to have the ability to calm your nerves, give yourself a confident boost and dial down pain on command. How about finally kicking a bad habit for good? That is what self-hypnosis will enable you to do. Being able to hypnotize yourself out of or into any situation is to have the ability to harness the power of your mind to control your body – mind over matter. Wouldn't that be an incredible skill to have?

Don't get me wrong; it is a good idea to visit a hypnotherapist, especially if you need is great and could use expert guidance. There are also hypnotic audio tracks in the market with verbal guidance and sublime messaging that can aid you in conducting self-hypnosis, though it is they are not necessary for you to learn the techniques outlined here. You have absolutely nothing to lose! On top of that, if you choose to undergo hypnotherapy, self-hypnosis can be used to complement and enhance the treatment you are receiving, thus helping you to reach your objective faster. Plus, you will also be less reliant on your hypnotherapist.

Before we proceed further, I do have a few more precautionary measures you need to know. Firstly, keep in mind that hypnosis is in the end a sort of medical procedure. Just as there are certain medicines you shouldn't be taking without a doctor's prescription, there are certain issues you should never attempt to fix on your own without consulting a qualified hypnotherapist.

If you have any of the following issues that need to be dealt with, and you believe hypnosis can help, do not under any circumstances use self-hypnosis. Please seek the assistance of a qualified hypnotherapist.

- **Interpersonal relationship problems.** If the issue you a facing involves other people – such as marital problems, trouble with family members or a misbehaving child – you may be in need of psychological counseling than hypnosis. There are areas in relationships that can benefit from hypnotherapy, but an objective evaluation by a neutral third party is needed to write an effective hypnotic script that can deal with the matter. An experience hypnotherapist may be able to help with this.

- **You have been diagnosed with mental illness recently.** A fragile emotional and mental state, especially if there is medication involved, may not the right the right frame of mind to be doing self-hypnosis without consulting a psychologist or psychiatrist.

- **You are experiencing symptoms that could indicate a serious illness.** Hypnosis can help with disease and pain management, but it is not a cure. If you suspect what causing you pains could be an indication of something physiological, see a doctor and get a proper diagnosis. Even if you are able to hypnotize the pain away, don't do that! The symptom is needed to make a proper diagnosis.

- **Uncovering hidden memories.** This is a very tricky area that only the most skilled and experienced hypnotist can competently tackle. Please don't go messing with your mind or you may end up with false memories.

- **You are unable to consistently practice self-hypnosis.** This last one is not so much a serious issue, but rather it has to do with your commitment with practicing self-hypnosis. As powerful f a tool as hypnosis can be, it is not going to work for you unless you practice. So, before you read on ahead, I want you to make sure you can fully commit to learning the techniques I'm about to teach. If your present life circumstances doesn't allow any room for consistent daily practice of self-hypnosis, comeback to this chapter later when it is more feasible for you.

Now that you know what areas you should never tread, let me tell you what you can best accomplish with self-hypnosis, and believe me there are plenty! You can use self-hypnosis with almost immediate success on any problem that fall into these two categories:

- Habit you truly wanted and are ready to give up or adopt

- You can think of a one-sentence suggestion to remedy this particular problem

A Word about Hypnotizing Others

Hypnosis is generally safe for most issues, aside from the aforementioned ones which you should only be conducted by a clinically trained hypnotist. However, you should never attempt to perform hypnosis on anyone while you are still in the learning stage. If you intent to use hypnosis to help friends and family, do so once you are able to easily perform self-hypnosis. I would not recommend trying to hypnotize anyone before you master the ability to hypnotize yourself.

Technically, all forms of hypnosis are self-hypnosis; the principles and practices are the same, whether you apply it to yourself or someone else. It goes without saying too that you should get the other person's willing participation, since hypnosis is a cooperative effort. You will learn how to hypnotize anyone in detail when you get to chapter 5.

Practice does Make Perfect

In a moment, I will go through with you how to induce hypnosis, then practice going in and out of a trance state. Remember, mastery comes from daily practice. I recommend you practice at least twice a day and keep a log of your self-hypnosis journey. Note down the time of each practice session, what you hope to accomplish, how the session go and the outcome. Of course, if you can practice more often in a day, you are encouraged to go ahead and do so.

The best suggestion I have for you is to set up a routine with your daily practice. Pick the times of day that is most convenient for you and stick with it for at least a month. You can practice in the morning as you are about to start your day, in the evening after work or at night before bedtime. What time you choose to practice does not matter. What's important is you stay on track. So, decide what's best for you and be committed to it.

Each self-hypnosis session takes only 10 minutes, which means you only need to allocate 20 minutes each day. When starting out, you want to practice in a safe and uninterrupted space. As you get better at inducing and coming out of hypnosis, it will take you a shorter time to go into a trance and you can gradually shorten your practice sessions to two minutes. Eventually, you will be able to go into a trance in less than a minute. When you reached that point, you will be able to practice anywhere, anytime. You could do a two-minute self-hypnosis on a bus or public space and no one will know it!

Once you become more proficient with the techniques, you will be able to go into a trance whenever there is something you need to accomplish with hypnosis. Are you ready to get started? Let's dive right into it!

Setting the Stage

To make the most of your practice session, you want to be sure to make the following preparations:

1. Find a quiet space where you can have privacy. Make sure that you will not be disturbed for the duration of you self-hypnosis session. That means turn off the TV and all electronic devices that buzzes and beeps, or at least get yourself out of earshot. Put your cell phone on mute (save for the timer function) and make sure

the kitchen stove is off. Make sure your practice space is well-ventilated too.

2. Have a timer ready. This shouldn't be a hassle as most smartphones come with a timer function. Just pick an alarm sound that is gentle, ideally a chime or tone. You don't want to be shocked out of a trance with one of those loud kitchen timer ringing sounds.

3. Be sure to wear loose and comfortable clothing. If you are wearing contact lenses, remove it, along with any dangling jewelry.

4. Now, find a restful spot where you can get your body into a comfortable position. This can be a bed, a reclining chair, a sofa or on the floor. Feel free to set yourself up on pillows or cushions.

Starting at Neutral

A hypnosis session consists of two parts, the induction and the input of suggestion. Right now, we will not be concerned with suggestions yet. You will practice inducing hypnosis first and how to deepen the state. You will be going into what is known as neutral hypnosis, a relaxed hypnotic state where no suggestions are given. Hypnosis with no suggestions is akin to meditation and does not solve any problems. We will get to the part about writing your own hypnotic scripts later. For now, I like you to experience what it's like being in a relaxed and suggestible state.

Whenever you are ready to begin, get yourself into a comfortable position, and set your timer for 10 minutes. Choose a spot to stare at. It can be a stain on the wall, a picture, something outside the window – anything will do. Then, follow these steps:

1. Stare at your chosen spot and take a few slow, long drawn out deep breaths.

2. As you fix your gaze on the chosen spot, tune inwards.

3. In your mind, tell yourself, "My body is getting warmer and warmer…"

4. Tell yourself, "My body is getting heavier and heavier…"

5. As you command your body to get into a relaxed state, really tune in and feel how warm, comfortable and heavy your body is becoming.

6. Allow every muscle of your body to let go and relax.

7. Tell yourself you, "I am in a state of deep relaxation. I am at peace and at rest."

8. Concentrate on feeling at ease and relaxed, while keeping your eyes fixed on the same spot. Keep staring…

9. Your hands and feet may feel a bit tingling. It is okay to wiggle them slightly, but keep your concentration fixated on the calm and rested feeling that is washing over you, spreading throughout your entire body.

10. Soon, your eyelids will start to flutter. Gently close your eyes and concentrate on whatever pleasant image that pops into you mind, or you can keep you mind blank and just be.

11. Stay in this state until the timer rings.

12. When you hear the timer, gently bring your awareness back to the room and open your eyes. Take your time and stretch out your body. You are now awakened from your hypnotic state.

So, how was it?

Depending on your degree of hypnosis talent, you may have experienced only brief relaxation on your first try. That is fine; just enjoy if for what it is and keep practicing. If you are among the highly hypnotizable, you would have felt the warmth and heaviness by the time you closed your eyes. Those with low talent for hypnosis may feel nothing happen and won't be able to close their eyes in the first few tries. It is also possible that you drift off to sleep. Once again, keep practicing! Make notes in your self-hypnosis log to monitor your progress.

Whenever you do the induction exercise, focus your thoughts on going into hypnosis, not getting out of it. Let the timer do the work for you. If you are worry that you will miss the timer and won't come out of a trance state, fear not! Let me assure you that no one can get stuck in a trance, because it's just not possible. You may drift into sleep while in trance, but you will always wake up at some point. Plus, being in a trance is a deliciously relaxed state that your body may want to stay in a while longer, especially if you've been stressed out. But it is not a state you can remain permanent in.

Stairway to a Trance

The hypnosis induction exercise outlined here is the simplest and fastest way to go into a trance, but I am going to give you another alternative here. You can practice both methods as you please to see which one works better for you. This method is not too different from the first one, but it adds a visualization component to the mix, to help induce a hypnotic state. You can also try to combine both methods, if that works for you.

As always, start by getting yourself into a comfortable position, set the timer for 10 minutes and make sure you will not be interrupted. Go ahead and take a few deep breaths to relax your body. Instead of starring at a chosen spot in the room, gently close your eyes and begin the inner dialog to tell your body to relax. Whenever you are ready, proceed in accordance to the following steps:

1. Create in your mind the image of a staircase, and see yourself standing on the bottom step, getting ready to ascend. Feel free to visualize your staircase however you want; it can be an old wooden staircase, a spiral staircase or an opulent one with bright lights and draped with carpet.

2. Tell yourself that you will count as you walk up. With each ascending step, you will go deeper into your mind and you will be deeply hypnotized when you reach the top.

3. See yourself walking up the staircase, one step at a time and with each step you take begin counting from one to 10.

4. When you reach 10m, you will be at the top of the stairs.

5. Create in your mind the perfect place where you can feel relaxed and be at peace with yourself. You can picture an outdoor scene or a beautiful room – it's up to you. Visualize it as best as you can. You can begin a count from one to five and with each number, let yourself see an additional detail in this imaginary space of your creation. Allow yourself to be absorbed and engrossed in the scene.

6. Remain in your visualized place and just be.

7. When you hear the timer ring, see yourself heading back to the top of the staircase and began to walk down. With each descending step, gently bring your awareness back to your body and physical space.

Let's Go Deeper!

If you have been consistently practicing your hypnosis induction, you can try to deepen the experience. To do this, you have to use the visualization method, but this time you have to engage all your senses. Don't just see the details of your mental imagery; hear feel, taste and smell them. Feel the stairs underneath your feet and the texture of the railings as you see yourself walking up. In your visualized scene, feel the air of the place, the scent, the ground beneath your feet and listen for the sounds around you. If you visualize yourself in a beach, for instance, tell yourself to feel the warmth sun, hear the waves crashing, feel the sand in your toes and smell the seawater.

Next Up, Writing Your Own Hypnotic Script

By now, I hope you are able to familiarize yourself with the process and experience of being in a hypnotic state. The next step is to use that state to reach whatever objective you have in mind. For that, you need to input the right kind of suggestions. Once you learn to say the right words at the right time, you will know what it is truly like to use mind over matter. I hope you will enjoy the process, because you are learning a skill that benefits you for life!

Chapter 4

Suggestions, Suggestions...

Under a hypnotic state, your guard is down and your mind welcomes suggestions. These suggestions go straight to your subconscious and will impact your actions without much effort. When you are able to use hypnosis effectively, goals like to quit smoking, exercise more, sleep better and be more confident in social situations will be attainable without much strive.

I trust that you have been easily able to get yourself into a relaxing trance state effortlessly. Perhaps you can do in and out of neutral hypnosis without the aid of a timer. So, you should be ready to start giving yourself suggestions. There are three ways you can accomplish this and I am going to go over them in detail. You may by now already have in mind the goals you want to achieve with hypnosis, but keep in mind that as wonderful a tool as it may be, it is doesn't work overnight. It would be wonderful if you can go into hypnosis and tell yourself all your problems will be gone when you wake up from a trance. I am sorry to disappoint, but that is not how hypnosis works. You need to know clearly what you want to work towards, and then come up with an action plan using hypnosis. Whenever you are ready to do that, read on.

Anatomy of a Suggestion

Hypnotic scripts can come in varying length, depending on your needs. It can be a single sentence, a few short sentences or a full narrative. Whatever the script length, all hypnotic scripts follow a general structure. Here is what's contained within a suggestion, in no particular order:

- The end goal

- The solution as a series of steps

- A specific command

Before you construct any kind of suggestion, be clear to yourself what exactly it is you want to achieve and how you plan on going about reaching your objective. Write that down in your hypnosis log. Always start with the end in mind and be specific. For example, if your goal is to lose weight, be clear how much weight you want to lose.

The examples given below are meant as guidance, and you don't have to follow the wordings exactly. So, feel free to adapt them to suit your particular situation and needs.

Quick and Concise Suggestions

I am going to start you off easy, with building a one or two-sentence suggestion. This type of suggestion is most effective when you want to quickly incorporate a new behavior into your daily routine that can contribute to your goal. It is the closest to a quick fix you have with hypnosis.

For the purpose of demonstrating, I am going to use two different cases as examples. Let's begin with the first example: the goal of being more physically active. You know that just taking a stroll at the nearby park for an hour, at least a few times a week, can work wonders for your sedentary lifestyle. Here is how you would create and use a suggestion:

1. Decide on an end goal (*Walk for an hour for four days a week*).

2. Think of one new behavior to achieve your goal. It should be something you do differently in your daily routine (*Spend less time sitting in front of the computer*).

3. What are two things you can do that will make it easier for you to follow through on the new behavior plan? (*Cut down on mindless internet surfing, and take a stroll at the park nearby*)

4. Write a sentence directing yourself to do the two things in Step 3. (*I will turn the computer off for an hour and I will use that time to take a stroll in the park.*)

5. Add the goal to your sentence. (*I will take a walk for four days a week, by turning off the computer for an hour and head to the park.*)

6. Add a specific command to your sentence, sort of an affirmative action. (*I will take a walk for four days a week, by turning off the computer for an hour and head to the park. Therefore, I will go to the park on the evening every Monday, Wednesday, Friday and Sunday, and I won't even check my social media during my walk*).

7. Once you have your suggestion created, induce hypnosis and say the sentences while you are in a hypnotic state. Feel free to repeat the suggestion as many times as you like. After saying it, visualize yourself doing what you just said. Take your time to really picture yourself accomplishing your objective. Your sessions can be as long or as short as you deem necessary.

8. Finally, add an affirmative statement and an awakening suggestion. Say it after you have clearly visualized having achieved your goal to gently bring yourself out of hypnosis. (*Now that I have absorbed the suggestions, I will bring attention back to my mind and body at a count of five and open my eyes.*)

You can use the created suggestion for as long as you need. As always, write it down in your hypnosis log. When you feel you have accomplished an objective and is ready to move on to another, you can start back at step one, perhaps set a goal that build on your previous one. Let's look at another example, using the same steps as outlined above, but this time for dealing with trouble falling asleep:

1. End goal: *To fall asleep easily.*

2. Decide on a new behavior: *Practice mindfulness meditation for 15 minutes a day.*

3. Two things to make it easy: *Listen to soothing instrumental music before bedtime and learn to just focus on own breath for 15 minutes.*

4. Give yourself directions: *Before I go to sleep each night, I will listen to soothing music and focus on nothing else but my breathing for 15 minutes.*

5. Add your objective: *I will fall asleep easily when I take time to listen to some soothing music and just focus on my breathing for 15 minutes before bedtime every night.*

6. Add a specific command: I will fall asleep easily when I take time to listen to some soothing music and just focus on my breathing for 15 minutes before bedtime every night. I will mediate lying down, so that it is easier for me to sleep after that.

7. Induce hypnosis, say suggestions and visualize the scene of success.

8. End the script and session with an awakening suggestion.

Script Your Solution

If you have a problem that is more complex, where layers of solution are needed, you can try using a longer script with a full narrative. The process of going into hypnosis and implanting suggestions is the same, except that a script will take a longer time to input and visualize. This approach is best utilized on emotional issues where you have no control over the situation, besides how to respond to it in the best way possible. For this example, I am going to use performance anxiety as the issue at hand.

Unless you make a living doing public speaking or performing on stage, it is understandable that nerves could get the better of you. The technique I'm about to described to you is commonly used in sports, where athletes are often taught to envision the perfect outcome for their performance. You can apply this method for any similar situation, whether it is to nail a public speaking engagement or keep your emotions from getting the better of you before an unpleasant confrontation. My one word of advice is to be prepared ahead, at least give yourself 24 hours before the event in question to do a self-hypnosis.

The hypnotic script you come up with should cover the following:

1. The problem

2. The solution

3. Steps to arrive at the solution. You want to keep this to three, at the most.

4. Visualizing the steps, one at a time, in great detail with all senses engaged

5. Visualizing the scene of success

6. Coming out of hypnosis

To start, take the time to think and write down specifically what is bothering you. State your problem clearly. In my example here, the problem statement is, "I am worried that my presentation on the company's latest product at the upcoming convention is not thorough and engaging enough." The solution could be, "I need to be well-prepared to make sure my audience is engaged."

Here is a sample script for preparing for a presentation:

Steps to the solution:

1. I will go over my plan for the presentation with the team leader to make sure I cover every key point.

2. I will rehearse my presentation with the team to boost my confidence.

3. I will ask for their honest feedback and areas I can improve on.

Next, induce hypnosis and visualize yourself carrying out the steps to your solution. Remember to not just see the scene like movie in your mind's eyes, but also feel, smell, hear and taste it. After that, visualize the scene of success in details.

Going by the above example, envision yourself stepping up to the podium and face the audience. You are calm and confident, ready to rock the show! Feel the cool air conditioning of the convention hall, taste the sip of water before you begin speaking and see yourself delivering your presentation, going through the slides one by one on the overhead projector. Hear the audience respond with laughter at the occasional joke you inserted along talking about your product. At the end of your presentation, you thank the audience and they applaud. As you exit the stage, your team comes by to congratulate you on a job well done. As you visualize all this, feel the sense of triumph that is rising up in you. Finally, end your session by saying your awakening suggestion to get yourself out of the trance.

Does hypnosis guarantee you success? Of course not, but it will definitely maximize your chances and prepare you mentally. Nothing can be worse than buckling under pressure and suffering an emotional meltdown before you even begin. With hypnosis, you aim to create a mental blueprint for success. If your blueprint is one of 'I cannot', what is the likelihood of the real situation manifesting in 'I can'? Just by using hypnosis to instill confidence in yourself, the battle is already half won.

Craft a Story

Ever watched a movie or read a book that simply has you hook on the story? Have you ever been inspired to action because of a story? Has a story ever make you question things your already know? You can't quite put a finger on it, but there is something about the story that just resonates with you. We are drawn to stories, more so than cold hard facts and statistics for a reason – a well-told tale is a form of indirect suggestion. The unconscious mind is wonderful at figuring things out on a symbolic level when the critical and analytical conscious mind doesn't interfere.

This last method of inputing suggestions is a rather advanced one, and would require more practice and preparation to implement. It also calls for you to stretch your imagination a bit to come up with a story, which also makes it the most interesting type of suggestion. Instead of giving yourself suggestions with directions and commands, you will tell yourself a metaphoric story under hypnosis, accompanied by visualization. Metaphoric stories are best used for cultivating a new belief, attitude or perspective. For instance, if you lack confidence and often feel awkward in social situations, perhaps you believe that because of the person you are, you will never be able to find love and acceptance, or you want to foster an attitude that can lead to improving your finances – these are the kinds of situations where a metaphoric story, when implemented repeatedly under hypnosis, would work best.

A metaphoric story is more effective if it is told to you by someone else who has a good understanding of your predicament and is able to come up with a story full of symbolism. That way, you can let the indirect suggestions sink in without thinking too much about them. In the following chapter, you will learn about hypnotizing others, where knowing how to create a metaphoric story will come in handy. If you want to give this approach to suggestions a go, there is certainly no harm in trying it out for yourself.

There are absolutely no rules for coming up with a metaphoric story, so you can just have fun with it! Start by thinking about the stories that inspire you, especially fairy tales and folklores, maybe revisit the books and movies you enjoy. Disney stories in particular are filled with symbolisms and characters that you can adopt.

I am going to give you a simple example for building confidence and self-motivation. Imagine you have a daunting task ahead that can only be described as an "uphill battle". It is definitely not an impossible feat for you to pull off, but it certainly poses a challenge you are never sure you would be able to overcome. You can use a steep mountain as a metaphor in your story. So, under hypnosis, visualize yourself at the base of a mountain, ready to run up to the top. Along the path, there are three obstacles in the form of a boulder blocking your way, a river to cross and a shaky bridge – each of them representing something that is holding you back. The boulder could represent limiting beliefs, the river can be social expectations and the bridge can be fear of failure.

You can add affirmative suggestions, such as, "I will clear whatever obstacles in my way. Success in inevitable for me." Then, visualize yourself running up the mountain path, stopping at each obstacle where you will find a way to overcome them. After clearing each obstacle, you arrive at a grand palace at the top of the mountain, where someone is waiting there to greet you. Because this is your own story, that person can be anyone – someone you know, a metaphorical figure for how you're feeling, a fictional character or ever your future self! What would this person say to you? What reward would they bestow upon you for your efforts? That's entirely up to you to decide.

To end your session, you can reaffirm your objective, followed by your awakening suggestion. You can word it something along the lines of, "I have removed all obstacles along my way to success. On the count of five, I will bring the attention back to my mind and body."

Make Your Own Hypnosis Tapes

Now that you know how to create suggestions, I am going to teach you another step to make your self-hypnosis process easier. The easiest way to give yourself suggestions when hypnotized is of course to memorize the script you have created for yourself before go into a hypnotic state, and then say it to yourself when you are under. This works best when the suggestion is short, but it can be a bit challenging if you want to work with a longer script. In that case, you can record your voice reciting the script and play it to yourself. Thanks to the voice recording function in most cell phones, you can record audio and have it uploaded to your computer or mp3 player.

Creating your own hypnosis tapes requires some planning, and if you are not used to speaking into a voice recorder, it could take some practice and trial-and-error. I highly recommend that you work with a properly written script. Most hypnotic audio tracks available in the market have a running time of 30 minutes to an hour, and guide the listener from start to finish. So, if you plan on making your own hypnosis tapes, write a full script for the entire hypnosis session, including induction, suggestion, and visualization guide and reawakening, then record it. Use a low, soothing tone of voice.

Be Patient and Keep Practicing

It is my sincere hope that at this point you are able to use hypnosis to help accomplish something you never thought possible. Even if you have made noticeable strides in trying to overcome a longstanding problem since you begin learning self-hypnosis, give yourself a pat on the back because you are clearly well on your way! If you feel you are not making any progress, don't give up! Hypnosis is not a push-button cure. It may take some time to gain mastery over your mind, but the effort will be worth it.

Chapter 5

Helping out with Hypnosis

If you have been following through with all the guidelines I have given thus far and have been practicing diligently, you most likely have experienced the amazing benefits of hypnosis firsthand. As such, you are probably eager to share your newfound skill with others whom you believe could use a helping hand. Before you talk someone into allowing you to perform hypnosis on them, I like you to take a moment and consider a few things as precaution. I am also going to touch on some ethics of hypnotizing someone.

Firstly, let me reiterate that all hypnosis is self-hypnosis. More specifically, a person has to want to be hypnotized first, for whatever reason. The role of a hypnotist is just to facilitate the process of getting a person under and then delivering the right suggestions. To be hypnotized by someone means you expand less effort and focus on inducing the entire process, thus allowing yourself to relax into it. By now it should already be clear that you cannot overwrite a person's freewill, no can you go against their personal values and beliefs. Hence, the number one rule to keep in mind when performing hypnosis on someone is to not give suggestions that goes against a person's objective. They are going to know it and stop participating, and there is a high likelihood they will never trust you again.

Secondly, I should remind you again of the don'ts listed in chapter 3. Unless you get trained and become a certified hypnotherapist, don ever attempt to hypnotized anyone with mental or physical illness, people going through relationship troubles, and definitely don't go digging around someone's memory bank. This can possibly lead to dangerous consequences you don't want to be bearing the brunt of. So, what can a budding hypnotist help out? My advice would be stick to the harmless stuff. You can help a friend or family member quit smoking, master a skill, calm their nerves in stressful situations or help them ease pain while getting a tattoo. The rule of thumb is, if a doctor is not needed, you can help. The steps for hypnotizing someone is the same as the ones for self-hypnosis outline in chapters 3 and 4. The difference here is instead of getting yourself into a trance state, you will be giving the instructions to guide another person into that state.

Lastly, find a willing participant who really wants to be hypnotized. This should go without saying, so don't simply try to hypnotize someone just to prove you can do it. More importantly, do not attempt to manipulate and mislead someone into consenting to be hypnotized by you. You are already crossing the line of what is ethical! A prerequisite to hypnotizing someone – or seeking someone to hypnotize you, for that matter – is to build mutual trust.

So, once you found a willing participant, be sure to go through these few preliminaries with the person before you begin:

- **Let them know what to expect.** Your participant may still be harboring misconceptions about hypnosis. Take it upon yourself to easy their fears and worries by giving them a crash course in what hypnosis is and isn't. Explain how they will fell when they are put in a trance, based on your own experience with self-hypnosis. They will be more open to it after their minds have been set at ease.

- **Have they been hypnotized before?** If they have experience with being hypnotized, ask them what was it for, how they feel about it, what it was like, what suggestions they were given and what was the outcome. This can help you understand what how hypnotizable they are and what they will respond to.

- **What are they looking to achieve with hypnosis?** Is their goal a better night's sleep? To manage anxiety and overthinking? To stay on track with their weight loss goals? Talk it out with your hypnosis partner, discuss possible solutions and use that information to create a suggestion.

After you have covered all the basics and have your script ready, find a quiet pace and get rid of all distractions. Once your partner is ready, you can proceed accordingly by inducing hypnosis and give suggestion as outlined in chapter 3 and 4.

Unlike performing self-hypnosis though, when you guide someone to go under, you can either remain silent for a few minutes and just let them absorb the suggestions given, or talk them through what to visualize after inputting the verbal suggestions. This will have to depend on what your subject is comfortable with, and should be something you work out together, perhaps involving some trial-and-error. If you are guiding them through creative visualization, remember to prompt your subject to engage all their senses. So, in addition to telling them "You see yourself doing....", also tell them what they would smell, hear, touch and taste – don't just paint the full picture, but transport them to another place and time. When you are finished, gently bring them out of a trance with an awakening suggestion.

After your subject has awakened from a trance, have a post-hypnosis conversation on the experience, asked them how they feel and get feedback on your performance as a hypnotist. Would they let themselves be hypnotized by you again? Do they have any suggestions of how you can better help them out? Your subject may have ideas for hypnotic script they want to try. Be sure to note things down in your log.

Pass on the Good Stuff

What can be a better way to improve yourself that by teaching others? Not only are you doing others a favor by teaching them a useful skill they can use to help themselves, you can learn from them and refining your own abilities along the way. If you are looking to try out hypnotizing others, perhaps you want to consider finding a participant who is also keen on learning the art, someone who can be your hypnosis buddy. Once you've successfully perform hypnosis on your subject, ask them to hypnotize you the next time. Learning hypnosis on your own is fun and rewarding, but it's even better when you have a study partner!

The Dark Side of Hypnosis

As you continue to explore the art of hypnosis and use it to enhance your life and that of others', I want to address a shadier side which I believe anyone who has dabbled in the art should be aware of. I am referring to the use of hypnosis for entertainment and other devious purposes.

Let's start with the one many of us are familiar with: stage hypnosis. In 2015, stage hypnosis Chris Jones appeared on the talent show, America's Got Talent. Judge Howie Mandel agreed to be hypnotized by Jones as part of the act. Mandel suffers from a severe germaphobia due to his Obsessive

Compulsive Disorder (OCD), and is known for refusing to shake hands. Jones wowed the audience by hypnotizing Mandel and made the talent judge shook hands with him and three other fellow judges. Jones gave Mandel the suggestion that everyone is wearing thin latex gloves that is barely visible (which no one is). Upon watching the playback, Mandel was mortified and publicly admitted to going for therapy after the incident.

Now, had Mandel gone to a hypnotherapist, he would be hypnotized to think that the human hands are not to be feared, that they are not pantry dishes for germs as his mental disorder had caused him to irrationally fear. It would have taken a few sessions of hypnotherapy to treat Mandel of his condition by stripping away layers of irrational fear, instead of tricking his mind into thinking everyone around him had invisible gloves on until he comes out of the trance.

Skeptics would call stage hypnosis fake, staged just for entertainment, and that both hypnotist and "volunteer" are in cahoots. You're not too far away from the truth. There are stage hypnosis shows that are entirely set up. However, there are people such as Jones who perform hypnosis on stage without trickery for the purpose of entertainment.

A stage hypnotist would cherry pick their audience for the most hypnotizable ones. They do this by giving the audience a suggestibility test – a brief induction followed by a simple suggestion to spot those who respond to simple indirect suggestion, using permissive language. For example, the moment the hypnotist steps on stage, they will ask the audience to close their eyes and say something along the lines of, "You can close your eyes now. Come one, just close your eyes and listen to me. Your eyelids will shut and remain shut, because they are too heavy to open. The more you try to open your eyes, the heavier they'll feel and the more they will remain shut." When they see audience members who are unable to open their eyes, they would know who to call up on stage.

Is stage hypnosis dangerous? Many academic and clinical hypnotists think so. These entertainers have no concern over the well-being of their subjects and are more interested in eliciting a reaction from the audience. Unlike healthcare professionals who use hypnosis in their clinical practice, stage hypnotists don't carefully word their suggestion in a way that is safe and beneficial to the participant. If you go to a clinical hypnotherapist, you will be told up front what sort of suggestions you are going to receive before being hypnotized. With a stage hypnotist, you are at their mercy the moment you allow yourself to be put under. Worst of all, this form of hypnosis continues to enforce the negative misconceptions about the art, so that those who are exposed to it become fearful and never get to realize the many benefits hypnosis has to offer.

But that's not all! There is a more sinister use for hypnosis where the hypnotists use subtle coercive tactics to get victims to consent to being hypnotized by them. This is the tactic of psychopaths whose aim is to keep their victims attached to them, before they begin the cycle of control and abuse. They would carefully target the emotionally vulnerable and then proceed to charm their victim, bombarding them with love and affection. Slowly, they will set up situations to gain the person's trust and cooperation, before putting them in a trance they are not even aware they had consented to.

It is worth knowing about these forms of hypnosis to safeguard yourself from becoming a reluctant participant, and to of course, to refrain from practicing them yourself. Now that you are armed with the knowledge of how hypnosis works, you should be able to protect yourself by identifying hypnotic language. Simply refuse to comply with hokey instructions or give in to permissive language. If someone strikes up a conversation with you and randomly say things like "Allow yourself to relax...", be on the alert and call them out on their trick! Hypnosis should never be used for entertainment and to victimize others. You never know what kind of damage you would be doing.

Leave the Kids Alone

Hypnosis is generally a safe, noninvasive therapeutic approach for anyone, regardless of age. As a budding hypnotist, however, do not attempt to perform hypnosis on children under the age of 13. You may think that since it is harmless, why not use your newfound skills to help out a kid who has trouble learning or to get them to stop biting their nails? I would strongly advice you against it.

Children cannot make the judgment to willingly participate in hypnosis. Because they lack the kind of intellectual resistance that adults have, children are normally a lot more highly susceptible to suggestions. You don't want to be implanting something into a child's mind that could lead to a host of problems for them down the line. Furthermore, a child may be having a problem that cannot be treated with hypnosis. I mentioned in the first chapter that our earliest contact encounter with hypnotic communication is through our parents. Indeed, parents may have unknowingly hypnotized their children into believing the world is a dangerous place, or they could have produce fearless and optimistic children. Words are very powerful to a child's impressionable mind.

In the clinical practice of hypnosis, children have been successfully treated for a myriad of problems like bedwetting, temper tantrums and recurring nightmares. If you have or know of a child you think can benefit from hypnosis, take them to see a hypnotherapist to be properly assessed and treated. A hypnotherapist may even teach parents and guardians hypnotic techniques and suggestion to help a child manage a problem. So, you are better off leaving kids to the experts.

With that said, it would do no hard to teach kids one-line suggestions as self-affirmations, if it helps them cope with a problem. For instance, if a child is often upset by being call names at school, you can say to him or her something along the lines of, "When people say things to you that makes you unhappy, you will ignore them and walk away." Just do not attempt to put a child in a trance on your own unless you receive proper training.

Chapter 6

Practical Applications for Hypnosis

The breadth of things you can accomplish with hypnosis is too much for this alone book to cover, Plus, as I mentioned in earlier chapters, there are certain areas that are not safe for amateur hypnotists to explore. Still, with a little creative thought, there is plenty of stuff you can accomplish with hypnosis with the bare basic skills.

In this chapter, I am giving you some sample hypnotic scripts for dealing with some of the most practical issues that most of us face at some point in our everyday life. They are divided into five categories – sleep, eliminating bad habits, picking up good habits, dealing with worries and fears and pain management. Many of the problems that fall into those categories are linked in some way.

I use specific case examples for each script, and I also include blank templates for you to create your own script in the form of worksheets. You are free to lengthen or shorten the script as you pleased, and modify them as you see fit. Feel free to play around with the wording. There are no hard and fast rules besides what works for you. I have written these suggestions in the first person. Just change up the pronouns to either first or second person accordingly, depending on whether you a self-hypnotizing or performing hypnosis on someone else. If you know it is going to take you a while to work through an issue with hypnosis and you would need to repeat a script, you may want to think about creating hypnosis tapes for repeated listening. I highly recommend that you use a combination of verbal suggestions and creative visualizations. So, follow up each verbal suggestion with a creative visualization exercise.

Plan of Action

Whatever you need to accomplish or work on, always have a plan before you begin. It bears reminding that hypnosis is not magic. You cannot hypnotize yourself into a slim figure, nor can your bank balance increase with each trance you enter. All of us would wish life is that easy, but hey, that's not how it works! So, have an action plan lay out that includes hypnosis where it matters to make sure your plan sticks. Hypnosis should be an item in your plan, used in compliment to other means, and not as the entire solution.

The key to coming up with a good plan is to fully understand your situation, what would jeopardize your efforts at a solution and what you need to do to overcome the issue in question. For example, if you have trouble losing weight, what is the underlying cause? Is it something critical like hormonal imbalance? If so, hypnosis can wait because you need to see a doctor. If the problem stems from your own lack of willpower or other lifestyle factors within your control, take a long hard look at yourself to find out what's wrong. Is it because you can't stick to an exercise program for more than two weeks? Can resist snacking after midnight? Then, it's time to write a hypnotic script to help with that.

Sleepless Nights

I want to give special attention to sleep, because sleep deprivation is a problem many of us have faced at some point, as the result of our hectic and technology-saturated lifestyle. If you habitually scroll through your social media feed for hours when lying in bed at night, you know what I am talking about.

Sleep is like hunger. It is as integral to our bodies as calories from food. Your body cannot do with insufficiency for optimal functioning. Plenty of studies have linked all kinds of mental and physical illness to regular sleep deprivation. Yet, many people keep taking quality sleep for granted. Fortunately, hypnosis is one of the most effective remedies for insomnia.

Start by taking notes of your sleeping habits. What time do you normally go to sleep? What do you usually do when you go to sleep? Hypnosis works best when you have a good sleep ritual in place. This is when you get into a routine of preparing yourself for sleep, including turning off all light and sound emitting gadgets, brush your teeth, do your nightly skincare regime, and change into comfortable clothes. You want to remove all sleep saboteurs.

Here is a sample script for those who have trouble going to sleep and staying asleep:

- *I will fall asleep easily and stay asleep for the next seven-eight hours, except when I must wake up during the night. If that happens, I will easily go back to sleep as soon as my head hits the pillow.*

- *I will ignore all minor noises, and sleep through them.*

- *As soon as I get into bed, I will move my body into the most comfortable position. Whatever move I make can be a cue for a restful sleep.*

- *My previous nightmare is gone and will never return. From tonight onwards, my dreams will be pleasant.* (suggestion for being awakened by recurring nightmare)

- *I will awake from a good night's sleep, feeling refreshed and rejuvenated.*

Visualize yourself entering your bedroom, and take note of the familiar furniture as they are in reality. See yourself walk over to the bed and lie down in the most comfortable position, pulling your covers over you. Feel at peace with yourself. Then, take a look at the clock and notice the time (you can also visualize looking at time on your smartphone, as most of us usually do these days). The time you see in your visualization should be the time you are aiming to go to bed every night. Once again, feel a deep sense of calmness and serenity wash over you as you get ready to fall asleep. You may say to yourself, "*I will get a good restful sleep and remain asleep, until it is the right time for me to wake up.*" As usual, end you session with the awakening suggestion.

I find hypnosis for overcoming sleeplessness to be most helpful when done lying in bed, just before actual bedtime, especially if you suffer from insomnia. If you drift off to sleep during hypnosis, just allow yourself to, though it is not the goal of the session. If not, as soon as you come out of a hypnotic state, you can proceed to rest and let yourself actually fall asleep. Do this a few nights to condition yourself to maintain a healthy sleep pattern and insomnia will be history!

Kicking Detrimental Habits and Addictions

If you ever tried kicking a bad habit, only to fall back into it a few days later, I can understand your frustration. Old habits die hard. I might as well tell you this upfront, trying to quit a habit cold turkey rarely works in the long-run. Your will power is not to be blamed though. It's just the paradoxical nature of your mind – what you resist persist. It's ironic to actually think about it, but when you actively think about not thinking of something, you end up letting it occupy your mind even more!

There will come a time when you have to address the bad habit and addictions, or else it will grow out of hand and adversely affect your life. Instead of throwing in the towel because your past efforts have failed, there's still hope! I am here to propose a more sensible action plan. So, take out your log book and write down the following:

- State the habit or addictive behavior you want to quit

- What can you do as a substitute to curb a craving?

- Make a list of activities that can distract you from giving in to the habit or addiction

- List down behavior and activities to eliminate because they lead to the bad habit or addiction

Once you have all that sorted out, try incorporating them into your hypnotic script. Now, here is an example script to quit smoking:

- *I will take / have a candy to get rid of a craving.*

- *I will drink water to banish a craving.*

- *I will get to working on my calligraphy practice and spend my time focusing on improving myself.*

- *Whenever I see smokers, I will feel sorry for them, because they are still smoking and I am an ex-smoker.*

Achieving the Unattainable

In a sense, trying to accomplish a goal is a matter of dealing with habits. You want to ditch the bad ones and cultivate the good ones. Understandably, trying to pick up a good habit and make sure it stays can be equally frustrating as trying to drop a bad habit and make sure it doesn't comeback. Never fear! Hypnosis is here to help! Whether you are trying to lose weight, master a new skill or perform better at work, with the right suggestions, you can reprogram your mind.

As always, be clear with what you want to achieve. As mentioned in chapter 3, you should start with the end in mind, and then reverse engineer the attainment process by thinking about the steps necessary to get your destination. Make a list of what can help or hinder your progress, and make a script out of them. For this example, I am going to use a common problem people have: building a habit of exercising.

- *I am in charge of my body.*

- *I can change my body to the ideal shape I have always wanted, slim, fit and healthy.*

- *I want to take better care of myself, because my health matters a lot to me.*

- *Every day, after I come home from work, I will dedicate an hour at the gym to improve my appearance and health.*

- *I look forward to my workouts each day, because I feel a small sense of accomplishment after each session, knowing that I have made more progress towards my fitness goals.*

- *With each workout session, I am a bit fitter and healthier than I was before.*

Follow up the suggestions by visualizing yourself exercising, going through the program as planned and then being able to fit into nice clothes. Envision having achieved the perfect body shape you want.

Curb Overthinking and Irrational Fear

Anxiety can have a debilitating effect on your overall quality of life, and if you are a worrywart, you may want to address the problem before it worsens into a mental disorder with physical symptoms. So, if you find yourself often preoccupied with something to the point of your palms become suddenly clammy and your heart rate goes up, take a moment to assess your concerns. If there is something you can do that will put your worries at ease, do it as soon as possible. More often than not, people get anxious from worrying about things beyond their control, which are usually not as bad as they thought.

Let's use hypnosis to reframe whatever that's keeping you up at night! This sample script deals with a common problem: money. Specifically, it deals with the fear or not being able to meet an important financial obligation:

- *I will not think about my bills until I see them in the mail.*

- *Only on the day it arrives in my mailbox, I will go online and log into my bank account to make the payment directly.*

- *On the rare occasion I have insufficient funds to cover the payment, I will immediately borrow from my other savings account.*

- *I will always have enough money to pay my bills, with more than enough left to cover all my living expense after everything is paid off.*

Coping with Pain

Pain is warning sign that should not be taken lightly. It is your body's way of communicating to the mind that something is wrong and for most of the time, you should not take the signal lightly. Hypnosis has been proven to work wonders for pain management. However, this is territory you want to proceed with extreme caution. **You should never ever hypnotize away pain without knowing what that pain means to your body.** There is a chance it could be a symptom to a serious condition.

With that said, not all pain is useful and that is what the following hypnotic scripts are for. Before we go there, I am going to explain how hypnosis works on pain. Our brains produced natural painkillers known as endorphins – a.k.a. the happy hormone. This chemical naturally blocks the brain from reacting to pain. Endorphins are released into the brain as a response when we experience great pleasure – during exercise, sex, laughing when watching a comedy and even when listening to upbeat music. The right kinds of words have also been proven to trigger releases of endorphins, especially when heard in a hypnotic state.

Being in hypnosis puts your body in a relaxed state, and that already puts you at an advantage to deal with pain, even before any suggestions are given. As I have warned, you should never simply hypnotize away pain. So, the following scripts are best saved for harmless pain, including pain after surgery, during a wound recovery, pain following a dental procedure or pain during a tattoo. If your pain is related to a medical condition, make sure you have the word from a doctor that it is okay to hypnotize it away.

There are various pain control and management suggestion approaches used in the medical field, some of which can only be performed by a very skilled hypnotist and would not be wise for you to self-administer. I am going to give you two methods that are safe, easy to perform and sufficient for common pain management needs.

Analgesia Suggestions

This is the easiest and most effective direct suggestions for pain relief. If the condition causing you pain is temporary and all you have to do is tough it out for the recovery duration, try these suggestions when under hypnosis:

- *I will feel no pain…no pain at all….absolutely no pain at all…*

- *The pain will diminish. It is already diminishing now.*

- *Before I know it, the pain will be so vague and minor that I will not notice it at all.*

Pain transformation Suggestions

If the pain you are experiencing is more intense and prolonged, I'm talking about the kind that interferes with your day to day activities and keep you awake at night. You can use hypnosis to reframe your pain by turning it into something else. This method calls for a little metaphoric storytelling, or rather, visualizing. I'm going to give you some ideas here, but you will have to come up with your own script that will work for you. So, when you go under hypnosis, try anyone of these:

- Visualize your pain as something you can pull out from your body. If you feel prickly pain, visualize yourself pilling out pins from the painful spot. With each pin out, the pain diminishes a little. You will put the pins in a heavy wooden box, which you then throw into a bonfire or ocean, into oblivion.

- If you are experiencing a burning pain, try a suggestion where you see yourself dowsing the 'flame' that's causing you pain with cold water.

- If the pain is concentrated in one part of your body, imagine it drained out of your body as black clouds of smoke through your fingertips, toes and crown of head.

- If you are preparing for a temporary painful experience, such as getting a tattoo or piercing, visualize the spot as if it is made of wood and is impervious to pain.

Chapter 7

Suggestions Worksheets

- Short Suggestions Worksheet

- Detailed Suggestions Worksheet

- Kicking a Bad Habit Worksheet

- Developing a Good Habit for Goal Accomplishment Worksheet

- Stop Worrying Worksheet

Short Suggestions Worksheet

1. My end goal is

____

____

2. What I will have to do differently (my new behavior):

____

____

3. The two things that will make it easier for me to do it are:

1. ____

2. ____

4. I must do these two things to easily accomplish Step 3:

1. ____

2. ____

5. I will do what I listed in step 4 to accomplish my end goal:

____

____

6. I will add (your specific command):

____

____

Detailed Suggestions Worksheet

The problem:

____

____

The solution:

____

____

Steps to arrive at the solution:

   1. _______________________________________

   2. _______________________________________

   3. _______________________________________

Describe scene of success:

____

____

____

Awakening suggestion:

____

____

____

Kicking a Bad Habit Worksheet

I want to stop

____

____

The circumstances which I do

____

____

most often are:

  1. _______________________________________

  2. _______________________________________

  3. _______________________________________

Every time I think about doing

____

____

I will immediately think about

____

_______________________________________.

Every time I am about to do

____

____

I will immediately do

____

_________________________________ instead.

The following situations often cause me to fall into the habit:

1. _______________________________________

2. _______________________________________

3. _______________________________________

The first time I ever experienced

____

____

was in the following situation (describe situation in detail):

____

____

I can visualize the incident playing out in a different way, where I do not end up slipping into the bad habit:

____

____

____

I feel proud when I see myself

____

____

Developing a Good Habit for Goal Accomplishment Worksheet

My goal is

____

____

I will begin to

____

____

I can see myself doing

____

____

under the following circumstances:

____

____

____

Whenever I do

____

____

It will be a reminder to myself to do

____

____

Stop Worrying Worksheet

My main worry is

____

____

Because of that, I am also worried about

____

____

Now, I am worried about:

1. _______________________________

2. _______________________________

3. _______________________________

I have these worrying thoughts because of (list your concerns):

____

____

____

Possible solutions, answers and opposing ideas to my worries:

____

____

____

Conclusion

The phrase 'mind over matter' is hardly just a figure of speech. You probably know that by now, having learned and experienced one of the most powerful mental tools for yourself. Although we have come to the end of this volume, this should not mark the end of your hypnosis journey – it should be the beginning. There is plenty more to learn and discover when it comes to the practice. There are so many possibilities you can achieve with hypnosis.

It is my sincere wish that this book have equipped you with a strong foundation of basic hypnosis skills, and have intrigued you enough with the practice to continue on the journey. You are just starting to tap into your potential, not just as a hypnotist, but also what you stand to accomplish in life with such a powerful tool at your disposal. Remember that mastering hypnosis is gaining mastery of your mind. For the first time now, you will be able to overcome the phobia you thought were unconquerable, you can now put yourself to the task to learn skills and achieve objectives you once thought were beyond your grasp. Hypnosis is about working to reshape your mental blueprint to the way you want. It gives you the power to undo any external influences that had taken root in your mind, but does not serve your well-being. Do use this skill for your own good, and when given the chance, share your newfound ability to give others a helping hand.

I certainly encourage you to keep on learning, keep practicing and exploring the power of hypnosis. There are plenty of resources out there for various levels of proficiency. You may want to consider visiting a professional hypnosis or seek out a teacher. Wherever you go from here, I wish you all the best!